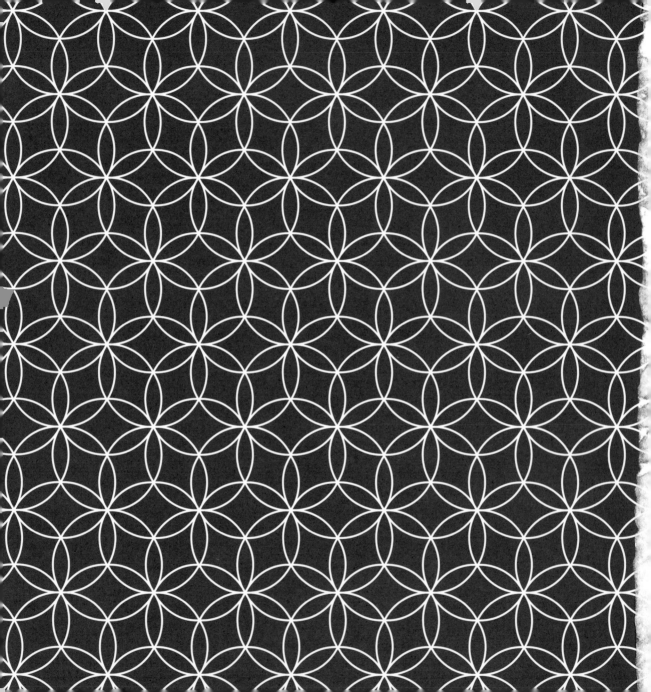

eat DRINK & Be

MARRIED

HERE'S HOW
this book
WORKS

Flip through until you find your favorite page
that hasn't been filled in yet.

Read the prompt all the way through.

In the blank spaces, write your words of love,
best advice, well wishes, or anything you want!

Feel free to make your entry serious, silly,
heartfelt, or funny—just be yourself!

When you're done, please sign your name
at the bottom of the page.

CONGRATULATIONS

....

There are so many people who couldn't be
happier and more excited for you! So, they've
written their advice and well wishes in this book
so you can refer to it when you need a good
laugh, a good reminder, and some good advice.

IF THERE'S ANY ADVICE
I CAN GIVE YOU ON THIS

SPECIAL DAY

I WANT TO TELL YOU BOTH TO ALWAYS

_____ even when

_____

_____.

And especially when _____

_____.

ALWAYS
MAKE TIME FOR

_____,

even when it seems _____.

Because really, is there anything better than

_____?

Don't forget to _____ before you

_____ and after you

_____ .

MY

BLESSING

FOR THE TWO OF YOU

IS THIS:

MAY YOU NEVER

_____ , _____ ,

or _____

and always _____

_____ .

LIFE
TOGETHER
· · · · · · · · · · · · · · · ·

will always be full of

_____ and _____,

as long as you always _____

and _____.

SOME SAY

LOVE

IS ALL YOU NEED.

But in my opinion,

_____

never hurts either.

ALWAYS

be sure to let your spouse know what you

_____

about them.

And don't try to _____

until it's the absolute right time!

IF YOU FEEL
you have to
CRITICIZE,

do it _____

and never _____ .

Because what's really important is

_____ .

TALK ABOUT
EVERYTHING!

Talk about _____,

_____,

and even _____!

NOW

IS THE TIME

to decide together

what a reasonable number of

_____

is okay to own!

Always let your love be stronger than

_____.

Your love is what will last!

NEVER

BOTH BE

_____

at the same time.

Don't think that all of your interests have to

be alike. It's okay to _____

_____

_____

_____ .

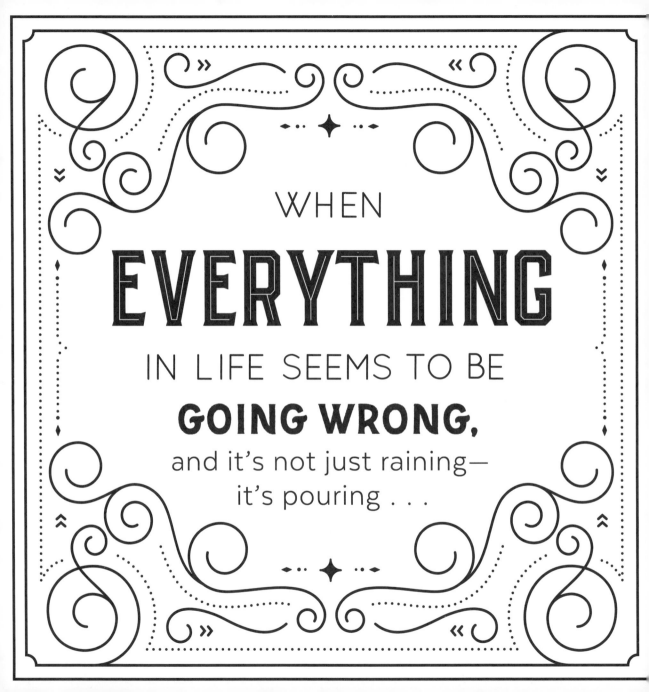

WHEN
EVERYTHING
IN LIFE SEEMS TO BE
GOING WRONG,
and it's not just raining—
it's pouring . . .

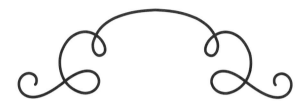

and it's hard to keep your chin up, always

_____

together.

LEARN HOW TO
ARGUE:

It's never a good idea to

_____ ,

as that will only make things worse.

But take time to really _____ .

ALWAYS,

always, always

pay more attention to your spouse than

to your _____.

A GOOD

MARRIAGE

IS LIKE GOOD

_____ .

It only gets better with time.

The couple that _____

together, stays together! Really, always find the time

to _____ with each other.

It doesn't matter, in the end, if

_____

or _____

happens. What matters is

_____.

THE
SECRET
to a happy marriage is

_____

_____

_____ .

At lease once every day, try to

_____, _____,

and _____.

WHEN I FOUND OUT YOU

TWO

were getting married, I

_____!

I've known you, _____,

for_____ years . . .

and I've known you,

_____,

for _____ . The two of you are perfect together!

My one piece of advice for you is this:

_____

_____

_____ .

✦

ALWAYS

TRY TO KEEP

your sense of humor when

_____

happens. And if _____

happens as well, try to just laugh through it!

KEEP

_____

_____

_____

at the center of your marriage.

TAKE THE
TIME

to nurture your relationship with a weekly

_____ .

My blessing for the two of you is this:

may you never _____,

_____, or

_____

and always _____

_____.

Some of the

CRAZIEST

advice I've ever heard was this:

_____.

But I think it's more important to

_____.

I BELIEVE THAT A
LASTING MARRIAGE

is built on three important things:

_____,

_____,

and _____.

One of my favorite things to do with

my spouse is _____.

It really helps us to remember

_____.

So, when you're both feeling

_____,

try _____.

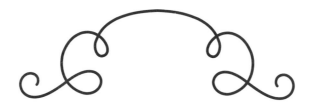

My best

ADVICE?

Never forget to

_____

before you _____!

AT

some point in your

MARRIAGE,

I recommend you take a romantic trip to

_____ .

. . . .

And when you're there,

make sure to _____,

eat _____,

and then _____

together when the day is done.

Don't let days go by where you forget to

_____

and _____

each other.

EXPRESS

your deepest

_____

and your wildest _____

with each other.

I think

RELATIONSHIPS

are made up of

20% _____ ,

10% _____ ,

5% _____ ,

and 65% _____ .

ALWAYS
TELL YOUR SPOUSE

_____

_____!

But, whatever you do, don't tell them

_____

_____.

For the perfect date night,
go stargazing or even

_____

together.

Some of the greatest

ADVICE

my _____

ever gave to me was this:

_____

_____

_____

_____.

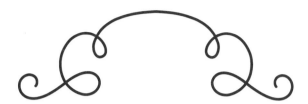

Be your spouse's biggest

_____,

not their biggest

_____.

I WANT TO
WISH YOU
nothing but

_____

for the rest of your life together!

I wish you endless amounts of

_____

and copious amounts of

_____ .

I WISH THAT

you'll always

_____

and never _____ .

I wish, above all else,
that you'll be

_____

together, from now until yesterday
and for all the tomorrows.

SHOW

YOUR APPRECIATION

for the other at least

_____

times per day.

SPENDING
TIME

together is just as important

as spending time apart because

_____

_____

_____.

CELEBRATE

every

_____

as a couple—no matter how big or small!

Never talk badly about your spouse to

_____.

Even if you may feel _____,

always _____.

SOMETIMES,
ONE OF YOU

may be _____

while the other one of you is

_____.

This is when it's important to

_____.

PRIORITIZE

_____

above all else.

_____ is what matters;

_____ doesn't.

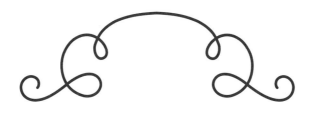

FOCUS

on being

_____

instead of being _____.

Don't take

LIFE

too _____

or else you'll miss out on all the

_____.

LEARN

to be silly together!

Never let a rainstorm go by without

_____,

and if you find yourself near a candy store,

always _____.

SWINGS?

Heck yes! Go sit on one and

_____.

Own any board games? Play them!

Play them in a park, in a _____,

or even in a _____!

RECREATE

YOUR FIRST

_____,

your second _____,

and your third _____.

REMEMBER

TO STAND BY EACH OTHER

when _____

but especially when

_____ .

If you don't have a

SONG

yet, find one!

And once you've found it, turn it on

when you _____,

when you _____,

and especially when you _____

_____.

Don't ever take your partner for granted.

Give your marriage the best chance of

success by never _____

and always _____.

You both should put just as much love,

_____ ,

effort, and _____

into your relationships as you did when

_____ .

Never

KEEP

your _____

habits from each other!

On your

FIRST

wedding anniversary, plan to

_____.

And don't forget to _____

as well!

NO MATTER WHAT

some people may say, disagreements

are okay and even healthy . . .

They
TEACH
you how to listen, how to

compromise, how to _____ ,

and how to _____ .

Learn how to argue with

_____ !

Learn how the two of you

_____ together.

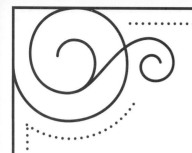

CHOOSE

TO LOVE EACH OTHER

every _____,

even when one of you may

_____.

HUG,

KISS, AND

_____

as often as you can!

TAKe YOUR

SPOUSE

for who they

_____

and not who you _____.

Always remember to say

" _____ ",

" _____ ",

and " _____ ".

I wish the two of you a lifetime full of

_____

and _____.

And also, maybe a vase full of

_____

and a bucket full of _____.

After many years of being married, you might

forget to _____

every once in a while. But don't let this go!

Always try to remember to

_____.

GIVE

your best selves to each other.

Grow together, _____

_____ together,

laugh together, _____

together, and most importantly,

learn together.

BE

_____

with each other, be kind with each other,

and be _____

with each other above all else.

LEARN
TO DISAGREE
without getting angry.

Learn to disagree without

_____

_____

_____.

L E A R N

to be respectful even when

_____.

Learn to stop the argument before

_____.

Learn to love, even when

_____.

IN MY RELATIONSHIP,

I've found that a tall glass of

_____ ,

a bowl full of _____ ,

and a good _____ movie

can really help lift the spirits when

the stress is high.

LEARN

the art of

_____

together.

Have the kind of marriage

that will encourage your sons to want

to grow up to be good

_____,

and your daughters to want to grow up to

be good _____.

----

can fix anything! Even the worst
of all arguments!

_____

will last forever;

_____,

will not.

LIFE

ISN'T ABOUT

_____

but about learning to

_____ instead .

Boundaries—they're a must!

No means no and _____

means _____.

It's really important to respect

_____.

Turn up the

TUNES

together!

I find that music is especially helpful

for when the two of you

_____ .

SING
TOGETHER

during _____.

Sing really loud when

_____.

Or, even roll the windows down in your car

and sing like _____!

LIFE

together can be really amazing or really bad!

It'll be amazing if you always remember to

_____.

And it'll be really bad if you

_____!

Learn to say, "You're _____

and I'm _____."

It's not always about being right— it's

about being _____

instead.

ALWAYS

just admit it when you're

_____.

NEVER

be afraid to say

_____.

HAVE

each other's backs when you

_____.

AND ALWAYS,

always remember to

_____.

ON ALL
of your
WEDDING

anniversaries, it's a super bad idea to

_____.

But I think it's a really good idea to

_____.

KISS

your spouse at least

four times per day: when they

_____,

when they _____,

when they _____,

and especially when they

_____.

SET

_____

expectations, celebrate the _____

things, have _____

while you can, and never stop being

_____ .

A lasting marriage is built on

_____

and _____ .

And maybe even a little bit of

_____ .

_____

_____

_____

at least once a day! No distractions.

No cell phones. Just the two of you!

Tell your

LOVE

STORY

to whoever will listen!

TELL IT TO

_____

and even to _____!

Sharing your own story will help the

both of you to remember

_____.

I really

BELIEVE

that the happiest couple

in the world doesn't necessarily have

_____

—they have _____ instead.

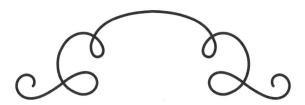

Always make sure

to treat each other with

_____,

love, _____,

and respect.

MY

_____

once told me

_____,

and this advice has helped me in my

relationship in so many ways.

You have to try

_____

together! Really, there's nothing quite like it.

It's _____.

And it's really really

_____!

Remember to be mindful

of each other during

_____

_____

_____ .

MAKE

yearly traditions together

for a holiday, or even just because!

Something my spouse and I do together

every year is _____

_____

_____ .

Try to show your love for each other

in times of _____

_____

and times of _____ .

ALWAYS

BE SURE TO

remind your spouse that not only do you

love them to the moon and back . . .

but that you also love them to the

_____

and back twenty times, to the furthest

reaches of _____

and back, and to the deepest parts of

_____ and back.

YOU TWO
make the cutest couple

I've ever seen! Like really, you both go together

like _____

and _____ .

Never forget to _____

together.

IT'S TOTALLY
okay to

_____

every once in a while. You don't always

need to feel the need to _____

_____!

If you find yourselves

falling into the same routine day after

day, try shaking things up a little by

_____ .

Always wanted to try _____

together but felt too _____?

No one has to know, so give it a shot already!

ALWAYS

try to hold on to that

first-date feeling. Remember when it

felt like there were not butterflies in your

stomach, but _____

were in there too? Grasp hold of that feeling

through times of _____ .

Recreate it by _____ .

Never let it _____ .

Here's to wishing you

_____

years of absolute _____,

_____ evenings filled with

_____,

cupboards and pantries full of

_____,

and a never-ending supply of

_____!

In my opinion, the secret

to a long and happy life together involves

a copious amount of _____.

But if one day you both find that the spark

between you is a little bit _____

_____,

just breath. It'll all be okay when

_____.

REALLY
DEVOTE
your time to finding

the best places to _____,

the craziest places to _____,

and the quietest places to _____

_____.

DO

_____ together.

Be _____ together.

See _____ together.

And always _____ together.

Looking for a date night idea at home?

Try writing love notes to each other!

Reminisce about some of the best

_____ you've shared,

or talk about your favorite

_____together . . .

or maybe even list the things

your partner does to make you feel

_____.

You could also think back to your

_____

and talk about how amazing it was!

I recommend

CREATING

your ultimate couple's bucket list together.
Maybe it could include going to

_____ ,

seeing _____ ,

watching _____ ,

or even _____ .

YOUR
LOVE
is timeless and

_____.

It knows no depth and it

_____.

It's inspiring and makes me believe

_____.

I wish I could use 20 pages just to tell you

_____,

but I'll just say this above all: Congratulations

_____ and _____!

I wish you both nothing less than a lifetime

full of _____.

I GOT TO SIGN
THE LAST PAGE!

And it's probably because I wanted to say
this to you both the most: I seriously couldn't
be more _____
for the two of you than I am right now.
The love that the both of you share makes
my heart _____,
and it reminds me to _____
_____
_____ .

GIBBS SMITH
TO ENRICH AND INSPIRE HUMANKIND

24 23 22 21 20   5 4 3 2 1

Written by Kenzie Lynne, © 2020 Gibbs Smith

Illustrated by Nicole LaRue, © 2020 Gibbs Smith

Published by
Gibbs Smith
P.O. Box 667
Layton, Utah 84041

1.800.835.4993 orders
www.gibbs-smith.com

Designed by Nicole LaRue

Printed and bound in China
Gibbs Smith books are printed on either recycled, 100% post-consumer waste, FSC-certified papers or on paper produced from sustainable PEFC-certified forest/controlled wood source. Learn more at www.pefc.org.

ISBN: 978-1-4236-5499-5